Animal Doctors

Angie Trius & Mark Doran
Julio Antonio Blasco

Laurence King Publishing

LAURENCE KING

Published in 2016 by
Laurence King Publishing Ltd
361–373 City Road
London EC1V 1LR
T +44 (0)20 7841 6900
F +44 (0)20 7841 6910
email: enquiries@laurenceking.com
www.laurenceking.com

A catalog record for this book
is available from the British Library

ISBN: 978 1 78067 832 0

Printed in China

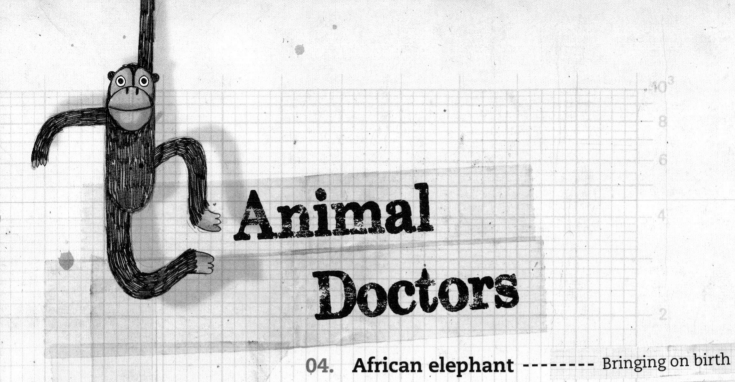

Animal Doctors

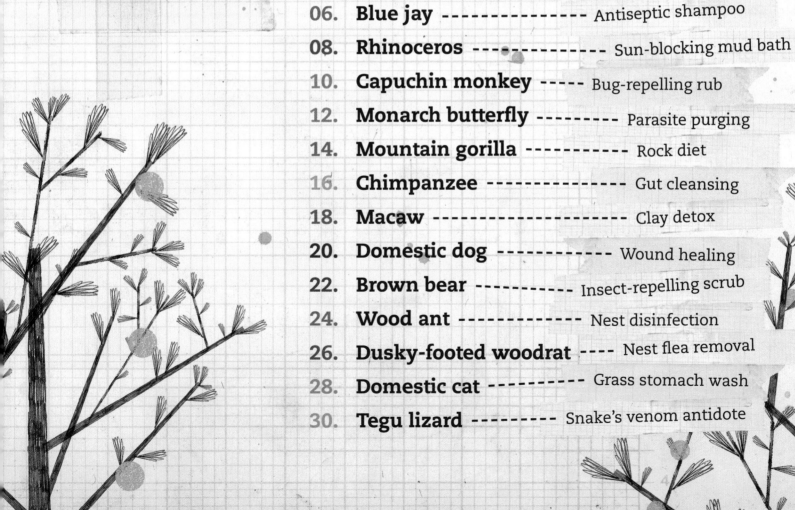

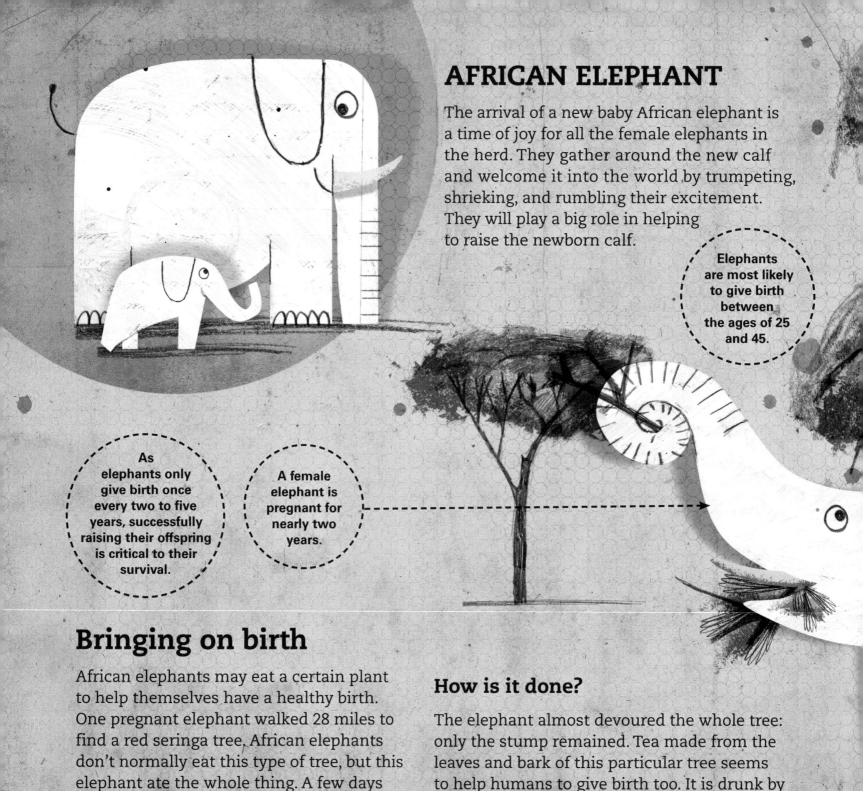

AFRICAN ELEPHANT

The arrival of a new baby African elephant is a time of joy for all the female elephants in the herd. They gather around the new calf and welcome it into the world by trumpeting, shrieking, and rumbling their excitement. They will play a big role in helping to raise the newborn calf.

Elephants are most likely to give birth between the ages of 25 and 45.

As elephants only give birth once every two to five years, successfully raising their offspring is critical to their survival.

A female elephant is pregnant for nearly two years.

Bringing on birth

African elephants may eat a certain plant to help themselves have a healthy birth. One pregnant elephant walked 28 miles to find a red seringa tree. African elephants don't normally eat this type of tree, but this elephant ate the whole thing. A few days later she gave birth to a healthy calf.

How is it done?

The elephant almost devoured the whole tree: only the stump remained. Tea made from the leaves and bark of this particular tree seems to help humans to give birth too. It is drunk by Kenyan women in order to kickstart the process of giving birth.

African elephant
Characteristics:

Shoulder height: 6½ to 13 feet.

Weight: 6,000 to 8,000 pounds.

Lifespan: Up to 70 years.

Habitat: African elephants are found in eastern, southern, and western Africa in dense forests, woodlands, or deserts.

Behavior: African elephants arrange themselves in family units. Each family is made up of around ten closely related females and their calves and is led by an older female known as the matriarch.

Feeding: Elephants use their trunks to pull off leaves and their tusks to tear off branches.

Enemies: Humans are the elephant's main enemy. They are hunted for their ivory and tusks.

BLUE JAY

The blue jay is one of over 200 species of birds that practice an unusual behavior known as anting. The bird places live stinging ants among its feathers.

Blue jays use their crests to communicate. An upright crest shows the bird is angry. If the crest sticks out in all directions the jay is scared. A flat crest shows the bird is relaxed.

The blue jay is known as a loud and aggressive bird.

Antiseptic shampoo

Stinging ants protect themselves from predators by excreting formic acid. Anting may help blue jays in two ways:

- The excreted formic acid acts as an antiseptic shampoo, keeping parasites in the bird's feathers under control.
- Once the ants have secreted all their formic acid, they become tastier and can be eaten.

How is it done?

Some jays will pick up ants in their beaks, rub the ant over their feathers, and then eat the ant. Others will open their wings and lie down over an active anthill, allowing ants to climb up on to them.

Blue jay
Characteristics:

Size: 10 to 12 inches from bill to tail.

Weight: 2½ to 3½ ounces.

Lifespan: seven years.

Habitat: Southern Canada and North America.

Behavior: Blue jays often have one partner for life and both help build the nest.

Feeding: Fruits, nuts, grains, and insects, but it is also known to feed on the eggs and young of other birds.

Enemies: Owls, hawks, snakes, cats, and other predators.

RHINOCEROS

Rhinos love wallowing in mud. But this favorite hobby is not instinctive, it must be learned. It is essential that rhino calves are trained to mud-wallow effectively, because it helps the rhinos in many different ways.

Two species of rhinos live in Africa: black rhinos and white rhinos. They both have gray skin.

Sun-blocking mud bath

Rhinos need to take good care of their skin. Despite the skin being half an inch thick, rhinos are sensitive creatures that suffer tremendously from sunburn and insect bites. Mud is a natural sun block, blocking dangerous UV rays. Because rhinos cannot sweat, a mud coating also helps to keep them cool. Mud also protects them from bugs.

How is it done?

When it is hot, it is critical that rhinos find hollows of muddy water where they can cool off. During the hotter parts of the day they can wallow in mud for up to two to three hours. They seem to enjoy a good mud soak.

Rhinos spend mornings and evenings grazing and only sleep during the hottest parts of the day.

Rhinoceros

Characteristics:

Height: 4½ to 6 feet.

Weight: Up to 5,000 pounds.

Lifespan: 35 to 50 years.

Habitat: Tropical and subtropical grasslands in parts of Africa.

Behavior: Though rhinos are often solitary, they do occasionally form groups called crashes. These groups are made up of a female and her offspring. A dominant male rules over an area of land.

Feeding: Rhinos are herbivores, which means they eat only plants and grasses.

Enemies: Young calves can be killed by lions, tigers, leopards, hyenas, wild dogs, and crocodiles, but humans are their worst enemy: through poaching and habitat destruction.

CAPUCHIN MONKEY

Capuchin monkeys get their name from the resemblance of their fur to the robes worn by monks of the Capuchin Order. They are some of the most intelligent monkeys and use tools as well as natural remedies.

Capuchin monkeys can communicate using different calls.

Bug-repelling rub

Capuchin monkeys rub their fur with at least four different plants carefully selected for their medicinal properties. Different parts of the plants are used, including seedpods, leaves, and the pulp and juice of fruits. This cocktail of chemicals helps the monkeys get rid of parasites such as lice, fleas, ticks, and mites.

How is it done?

Capuchin monkeys break up the selected plants with both their hands and mix them with saliva before rubbing the mixture over their bodies. Some of the plants contain chemicals that harm parasites. Others are used like lice combs to brush out bugs.

Capuchins are mostly diurnal and spend most of the day looking for food, except when they take their midday nap.

Capuchin monkey
Characteristics:

Height: 12 to 16 inches.

Weight: 5¾ to 9 pounds.

Lifespan: 30 years.

Habitat: Forests of Brazil and other parts of South and Central America.

Behavior: They tend to live in large groups of 10 to 30 individuals and one male dominates the group.

Feeding: Fruits, nuts, insects, leaves, plants, small birds, and other small animals such as frogs.

Enemies: Predators include jaguars, snakes, crocodiles, and birds of prey.

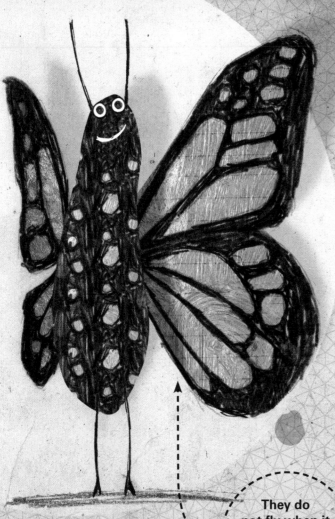

MONARCH BUTTERFLY

Monarch butterflies are well known for the incredibly long journeys they take when migrating from North America to Mexico each winter. They fly up to 3,000 miles! In their life cycle, they undergo a metamorphosis, from egg to caterpillar to chrysalis and, finally, to the adult butterfly.

Eating milkweed as a caterpillar causes the butterfly to store chemicals that make it taste horrible to predators.

They do not fly when it rains and retreat to shady places when too hot.

Parasite purging

Caterpillars (or larvae) are dependent on milkweed plants, which they eat almost exclusively. There are many species of milkweed but the scarlet milkweed is particularly high in chemicals called alkaloids, which have antiparasitic effects.

How is it done?

Adult monarch butterflies infected with parasites lay their eggs on antiparasitic milkweed plants to protect their offspring and prevent the infection being passed on.

Bright orange coloring warns predators that the butterfly is toxic to eat.

Monarch butterfly
Characteristics:

Wingspan: 3½ to 4¾ inches.

Weight: 0.0095 to 0.026 ounces.

Lifespan: Few weeks to 8 months.

Habitat: North and South America. Also found in Australia, New Zealand, and parts of Europe.

Behavior: They can produce four generations in one summer while migrating north. The fourth generation is the one that will migrate south for winter and lives the longest.

Feeding: Larvae eat milkweed plants, adults gather nectar.

Enemies: Global warming and habitat loss as well as pesticides that kill milkweed are their enemies.

Female gorillas give birth to one infant after a pregnancy of nearly nine months. Infants ride on their mothers' backs from the age of four months, until they are up to four years old.

Mountain gorillas have shorter arms than their lowland relatives.

MOUNTAIN GORILLA

Mountain gorillas are large apes that live in African forests high in the mountains, at up to 13,000 feet above sea level. They have thicker and denser fur compared to other gorillas to help them survive in a habitat where temperatures often drop below freezing.

Rock diet

Mountain gorillas eat plenty of high-protein plants and fruits when available, but at certain times of year their diet lacks essential minerals such as sodium, iron, calcium, and potassium. Eating rocks, soil, and dust can provide them with these nutrients. Clay in the soil may also help to keep their guts healthy by getting rid of toxins.

How is it done?

The gorillas loosen small pieces of rock with their teeth and grind them to a fine powder before eating it. They tend to do this more regularly in the dry season when their diet is poorer and contains more toxic plant chemicals.

Mountain gorilla
Characteristics:

Height: 4 to 6 feet standing.

Weight: 200 to 400 pounds.

Lifespan: 35 to 50 years.

Habitat: Forests and volcanic slopes in Africa (Rwanda, Uganda, and Republic of Congo).

Behavior: They live in groups of up to 30 individuals. These groups are led by one dominant male (called a silverback because of his gray hair) and include young males (blackbacks), females, and their offspring.

Feeding: Leaves, fruits, seeds, flowers, roots, shoots, and bark.

Enemies: Humans and leopards. They are critically endangered animals, with fewer than 900 individuals left in the wild.

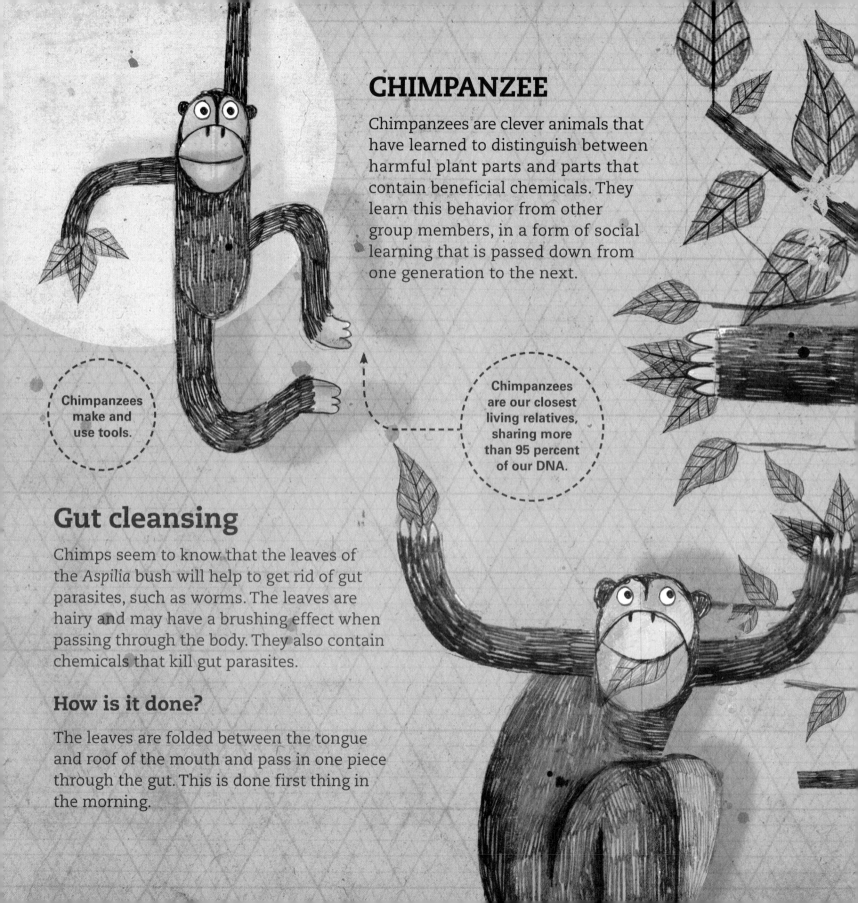

CHIMPANZEE

Chimpanzees are clever animals that have learned to distinguish between harmful plant parts and parts that contain beneficial chemicals. They learn this behavior from other group members, in a form of social learning that is passed down from one generation to the next.

Chimpanzees make and use tools.

Chimpanzees are our closest living relatives, sharing more than 95 percent of our DNA.

Gut cleansing

Chimps seem to know that the leaves of the *Aspilia* bush will help to get rid of gut parasites, such as worms. The leaves are hairy and may have a brushing effect when passing through the body. They also contain chemicals that kill gut parasites.

How is it done?

The leaves are folded between the tongue and roof of the mouth and pass in one piece through the gut. This is done first thing in the morning.

Chimpanzee
Characteristics:

Height: 4 to 5½ feet.

Weight: 65 to 130 pounds.

Lifespan: 45 years.

Habitat: African rain forests, woodlands, and grasslands.

Behavior: Chimps live in communities composed of family groups of 3 to 6 individuals, totaling about 50 animals. The adult males of the community, led by one dominant male, form hierarchies.

Feeding: Chimps are generally fruit and plant eaters, but they also consume insects, eggs, and meat.

Enemies: Habitat destruction is the greatest threat of the chimpanzee. Large population decreases are also blamed on hunting.

MACAW

Macaws (from the parrot family) are magnificently colored birds native to the rain forests of Central and South America. They are intelligent and social birds and they mate for life. Couples not only breed but share food and groom one another.

Their big curved beaks can crack nuts and seeds while their tongues have a bone, making them very useful for tapping into fruits.

Clay detox

Many plants and seeds eaten by macaws contain toxic substances produced by the plants for their own protection. To neutralize these toxins and clean out their bodies, macaws consume clay.

How is it done?

They gather on exposed riverbanks and lick clay on a daily basis. There is evidence that the clay is also consumed as a source of nutrients, particularly sodium, which is scarce in the foods they eat.

They vocalize to communicate and are great at mimicking human voices!

They are very loud, messy, and energetic.

Macaw
Characteristics:

Size: 12 to 40 inches from bill to tail.

Weight: 4½ ounces to 3½ pounds.

Lifespan: Up to 60 years.

Habitat: Central and South America.

Behavior: They are very social and often gather in flocks of 10 to 30 birds.

Feeding: Seeds, nuts, fruits, leaves, flowers, and stems.

Enemies: Snakes, monkeys, and birds of prey are predators of young parrots but adults have few enemies.

DOMESTIC DOG

Dogs are known as man's best friend. Humans and dogs have lived together for over 10,000 years. All dogs have a common ancestor in the South Asian wolf.

Dogs communicate by scent, vocally (barking), and by physical appearance: body position, movement, and expressions allow them to convey messages (like tail-wagging when happy).

Wound healing

Dog saliva can kill bacteria, just like an antibiotic. This means that the saliva can reduce the chance of infection and help wounds to heal. But do not allow dogs to lick your wounds as their saliva also carries bacteria that can be harmful to humans.

Dogs pant to regulate their body temperature, as they cannot sweat like us.

Domestic dog
Characteristics:

Height: 6 to 33 inches.

Weight: 2 to 175 pounds.

Lifespan: 12 to 14 years.

Habitat: Human households.

Behavior: They are very social. They defend their territories and mark them with their scent by peeing. They also bury bones and toys for future use.

Feeding: They like many foods but should stick to a balanced dog food diet.

Enemies: Humans are often their worst enemies but some wild predators can be dangerous to dogs, especially puppies.

How is it done?

Dogs lick their wounds to apply saliva. The saliva's antiseptic properties come from enzymes such as lysozyme. Additionally, the mechanical action of rubbing stimulates blood flow and improves the natural healing process. However, excessive licking can also cause problems, so vets often apply bandages or use collars to stop dogs from licking their wounds.

BROWN BEAR

Brown bears are the largest land-based predators on Earth and the most widely distributed bears in the world. They are solitary animals that live alone, except for females and their cubs. They eat all summer to gain weight for the long winter hibernation.

Insect-repelling scrub

Brown bears make a paste with osha roots (*Ligusticum porteri*) and saliva and rub it through their fur to repel insects or soothe insect bites. This plant, also known as bear root or bear medicine, contains many active chemicals, such as coumarins.

How is it done?

The bears chew the osha roots to make a paste and rub it into their fur by rolling on it and covering their bodies with its fragrance. Bears also tend to eat the roots when they come out of hibernation in order to cleanse their digestive systems.

Osha roots are native to the Rocky Mountains of North America. The name osha is believed to come from a Native American language and to mean "bear."

Male brown bears offer osha roots to female bears. To bears, it is like a romantic red rose!

Brown bear
Characteristics:

Height: 5 to 9 feet when standing.

Weight: 175 to 1,500 pounds.

Lifespan: 20 to 25 years.

Habitat: North America, Europe, and Asia.

Behavior: They hibernate for 5 to 6 months of the year so they need to eat a lot and store fat to survive all this time without food.

Feeding: Bears consume plants (berries, roots, grass) and meat (fish, insects, small animals, and carrion).

Enemies: Adult bears have no predators, but humans are a threat.

WOOD ANT

Wood ants are famous for their red and black coloring. They are a fascinating group with important roles in woodland ecosystems. They build large mounds as nests and these house huge colonies, which are made up mostly of females.

The combined weight of all ants would be about the same as the combined weight of all humans.

Nest disinfection

Wood ants harvest pine resin to keep their nests free from fungus and disease-causing bacteria. It is a remarkable example of preventive medication. A large nest can contain up to 45 pounds of resin.

How is it done?

The ants collect hardened sap from pine trees and carry it to their nest. The resin protects the larvae and the adult ants from infection. Ants have been observed bringing more resin to the nest when ant larvae are present. They position it around the larvae for protection.

Wood ant
Characteristics:

Size: ½ to ⅝ inch (queens), ⁵⁄₁₆ to ⁶⁄₁₆ inch (workers).

Lifespan: Up to 15 years (queens), workers up to 1 year (females), or only a few weeks (males).

Habitat: Woodlands and conifer plantations in Europe, North America, and parts of Asia.

Behavior: They live in colonies of around 100,000 workers and 100 queens. The nest is built from pine needles, soil, moss, twigs, and dried grass and it can be several feet high.

Feeding: Insects, including other ant species. They also farm honeydew (sticky, sugary liquid) from aphids. The aphids are stroked by the ants to make them release honeydew.

Enemies: They squirt formic acid to defend themselves against predators. Humans and deforestation are major threats.

DUSKY-FOOTED WOODRAT

Dusky-footed woodrats are small, brown, or gray colored rodents with dark feet and furry tails. They are nocturnal, having poor eyesight but an excellent sense of smell, touch (using their long whiskers), and hearing. Unlike other rat species, they usually live alone.

Rats have sharp teeth that grow constantly, so they chew on wood to keep them short and sharp.

Nest flea removal

Rats are very clean animals. They spend several hours each day grooming themselves. Dusky-footed woodrats place leaves from California bay trees around the edges of their nest to control fleas and other parasites like mites and ticks.

How is it done?

The rats nibble bay leaves to release strong-smelling chemicals inside. The chemicals are toxic to flea larvae.

They are particularly fond of shiny objects left behind by humans, and store collections of them in their nests.

Dusky-footed woodrat
Characteristics:

Length: 12 to 18 inches; half of this is the tail.

Weight: Up to 12 ounces.

Lifespan: 1 to 3 years.

Habitat: Oak woodlands and grasslands of North America.

Behavior: These rats live in nests built on rocky slopes or tree logs that can be more than a foot high. Adults generally live alone but share their territory with other woodrats.

Feeding: They eat seeds, flowers, fruits, plants, bark, and fungi.

Enemies: Snakes, wildcats, birds of prey, and coyotes.

DOMESTIC CAT

Domestic cats are small, furry felines and very popular pets. Their relationship with humans is ancient—Egyptians had already domesticated cats 4,000 years ago. They are fast and agile and spend many hours grooming themselves with their rough tongues.

Grass stomach wash

Cats are thought to eat grass to make themselves sick. This helps them vomit undigested food or furballs. Additionally, grass provides some nutrients and vitamins and cats like the taste.

How is it done?

Cats regurgitate the grass because they lack the enzymes to digest it. This means they can get rid of other undigested material in their stomach that might otherwise cause pain. This is especially important when cats eat prey with bones and feathers, which cannot be digested.

Cats have powerful night vision, as well as excellent hearing and a strong sense of smell.

Cats sleep for up to 70 percent of the day but when awake they can run up to 30 miles an hour.

Domestic cat
Characteristics:

Size: 28 inches.

Weight: 9 to 11 pounds.

Lifespan: 12 to 15 years.

Habitat: Human households.

Behavior: Cats need to scratch surfaces to sharpen their claws, but they also use this behavior to leave their scent behind.

Feeding: Cats are carnivores so they like meat and fish. They are natural hunters able to catch birds, mice, and other small animals.

Enemies: Natural enemies are foxes, coyotes, wolves, racoons, and sometimes dogs. None of these animals can climb like cats do!

TEGU LIZARD

Tegus are large and muscular lizards covered with raised, bumpy scales. They are very intelligent land animals. They use their forked tongues to "smell" the air and find food. They often hibernate during the colder months (September to March) when food is scarce.

Tegus are capable of destroying a beehive to get hold of honey. They have a sweet tooth!

Snake's venom antidote

When bitten by snakes, tegu lizards are known to eat the roots of certain plants. These plants are believed to contain chemicals that act as an antidote and neutralize the venom.

How is it done?

The tegu looks for the root of the *Jatropha* plant every time it is bitten by a snake. These plants are also used as a traditional medicine for the treatment of snake bites as well as other illnesses such as rheumatism.

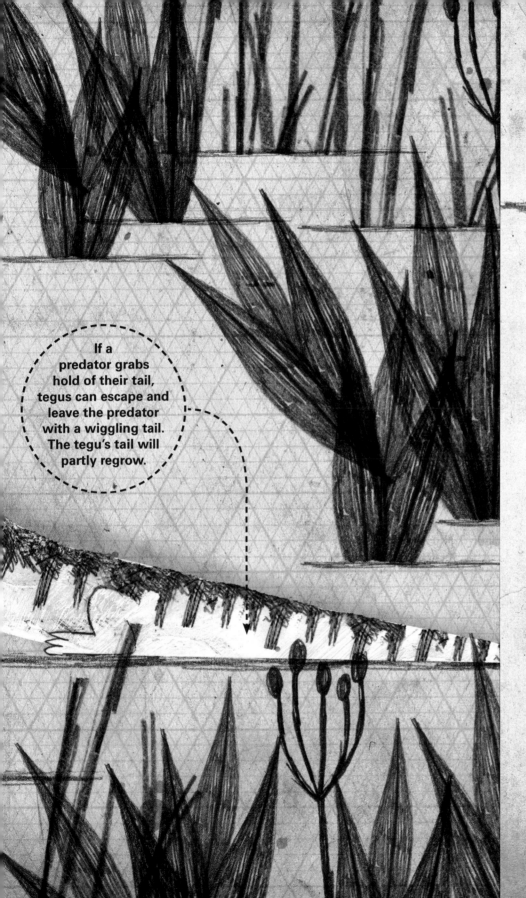

If a predator grabs hold of their tail, tegus can escape and leave the predator with a wiggling tail. The tegu's tail will partly regrow.

Tegu lizard
Characteristics:

Length: Up to 5 feet (males).

Weight: 22 pounds or more.

Lifespan: 15 to 20 years.

Habitat: South America.

Behavior: Their sharp teeth and strong jaws make it easy for them to chew through the toughest meat. The teeth are also handy for defending themselves, and they can use their tail as a whip.

Feeding: They eat plants, seeds, berries, fruits, small rodents, insects, eggs, amphibians, mollusks, and birds.

Enemies: Pumas, snakes, and birds of prey. Although tegus are not threatened, they are a favorite target of human hunters for food and the sale of their skins.

Angie Trius is a doctor in veterinary medicine with a special interest in food science and technology. She has worked in the area of food ingredients in the USA and Europe for more than 20 years. In 2002 she cofounded a small contract research company that provides worldwide technical expertise in the area of hydrocolloids.

Mark Doran is a consultant neurologist with a Chemistry degree and a PhD in quantum mechanics. He works in various hospitals in the UK and has more than 30 years experience in general neurology. Mark is a former senior lecturer in neurology at the University of Liverpool and Cambridge University. He has a passion for science research and the wide diffusion of science.

Julio Antonio Blasco was born in Valencia, Spain, where he graduated in Fine Arts. He is an illustrator and graphic designer and has published many children's books, some of which have won awards.

Since 2012 he has worked from his own studio on projects including illustrating books for both children and adults, as well as albums, catalogs, posters, games, exhibitions, and much more.

www.julioantonioblascolopez.com